MW01065338

DREAMS

HEARING THE VOICE OF GOD THROUGH DREAMS, VISIONS, AND THE PROPHETIC WORD

BY J.D. KALLMYER

MORIAH PRESS
Havre de Grace, MD 21078-0917

DREAMS: HEARING THE VOICE OF GOD THROUGH DREAMS, VISIONS, AND THE PROPHETIC WORD

Copyright © 1998 by J.D. Kallmyer

ISBN 0-9657682-1-X

Published by Moriah Press
P.O. Box 917
Havre de Grace, MD 21078-0917
(410) 939-9618

All rights reserved. No portion of this book may be reproduced in any form without the written permission of the Publisher.

Printed in the United States of America

DEDICATED TO

The intercessory prayer team
who the Lord used to inspire this book.

Diane Angelucci
Mary Briggeman
Liz Casey
Barbara Evans

AND MANY THANKS TO

Larry Evans who set aside valuable time to
proofread and edit the final manuscript.

Table of Contents

Preface

This book in your hands has been designed to use Scripture as the basis for teaching students of the Bible how to properly understand dreams and visions, and help determine when God may be using them as a vehicle to provide understanding or protection, or to protect, assure, exhort or caution the dreamer about some past, present or future event. It is my desire to bring balance to the study of dreams. As with all subjects touching the eternal, we must not be given to obsessive extremes and must always remain anchored in the Word of God. The key to unlocking the power of dreams from a biblical perspective is Jesus Christ. All revelation from God, across the expanse of time, from creation to Calvary to the coming millennial reign of our Lord and beyond, is focused in Him. If He is not exalted in the process, our efforts are fruitless and vain.

J.D. Kullmyer

Dreams are so intimate, so fantastic, that many dreamers are not surprised — and perhaps even secretly pleased — that dreams have proved so illusive to science.

George Howe Colt

1

The Field of Dreams

There stretches a world beyond our natural sight which reaches into infinity. It is densely populated and filled with intrigue. It is a world of gods and demigods; of magic and sorcery; and of wickedness and sensuous delight. But it is also a world of divine creativity in which an omnipotent God works out His will. In this vast world, there is great conflict.

The activities of the powers and principalities of darkness, and of the angels and archangels intersect with the material plane. Humans are provided with limited glimpses into the otherworld, where these beings interact. Indeed, what spirit creatures do, and why they do what they do, is integrally related, even dependent upon, the course of human events. Perhaps there is no place where an individual might gain a clearer look into this world than in the subconscious domain of sleep. If that be true, there is little wonder why the odd world of dreams and visions is so utterly fascinating and mysterious.

Through the ages, dreams have been a powerful source of meaning, an impetus for change, and have provided direction for young and old, rich and poor, and the powerful as well as powerless.

All people dream. Sometimes people remember them and sometimes they do not. Regardless, dreams are reflections — important reflections. To be sure, their significance moves beyond the temporal to the realm of the eternal God, His providential care for the created order, and the outworking of His divine plan for mankind.

The Apostle Paul remarked that unseen forces attempt to manipulate the stage upon which we find ourselves, including the platform of our dreams. Our battles, he said, are not "against flesh and blood, but against principalities, against powers, against the rulers of the darkness of this world, against spiritual wickedness in high places" (Eph. 6:12). Without special gifting, unholy alliances, or blind penetration, those unseen forces remain hidden from the mind's eye, especially during our waking hours. When our guard is down, they seem to appear with peculiar intensity.

While sleeping, the anchor of consciousness is lifted and the soul is swept into the currents of a world which often seems bizarre and alien. So strange are dreams that many disregard them as incomprehensible and not worth examining. People turn up on the dream stage whom the dreamer has never met. The geography can be foreign and the terrain challenging, forcing detours, and sudden changes in destination which, in turn, demand unexpected plot shifts. There occurs a juxtaposition of the familiar and strange — creatures appear, mutants, half man and half insect or part man and part beast. Often compressed and jumbled, dreams are sometimes disturbing and ominous, frequently mysterious, generally informative, but repeatedly too illusive and difficult to clearly comprehend.

Many people honestly believe they do not dream. Regardless, few know much about dreaming, Christians included. Other than occasionally sharing an unusual dream, little is said. Perhaps that is because the dreams that are remembered can be so absurd as to be totally incomprehensible. Often, the dreamer recalls only fragments — bits and snatches that are connected only by the dream itself. Then too, how much time do you want to spend examining a dream? Making sense of dreams involves an investment of energy that produces a pay-off that is too illusive to many would-be dream enthusiasts.

While the theology of dream interpretation is examined in detail in Chapter 4, I would be remiss in not emphasizing here that we must resist approaches which trivialize the subject. Anyone who suggests a "dream interpretation made simple" design is uninformed at best and downright deceitful at worse.

Clearly, Scripture reveals that the field of dreams is a domain Yahweh uses to perfect His will. For that reason alone, it has, since the beginning of time, been marked for penetration by the forces of darkness. And therein is our dilemma. For we who believe our dreams are an important bridge between God and man, how do we filter out the flotsam designed to obscure God's revelation to us? In order to accurately decipher our dreams, it is essential to begin with authentic data. The biggest obstacle to getting at the truth is the threat posed by assimilating counterfeit or garbled messages into the framework for making meaningful decisions. That statement is not intended to diminish the fact that rightly exposing the existence and meaning of

14

deceptive information can be extremely valuable in and of itself. Indeed, something important about the enemy's strategy might be revealed.

Dream researchers insist that only the dreamer can interpret his own dream. With this in mind, there seems to be as many techniques to interpret dreams as there are dreamers. There are no universal archetypes or dream images, say some. Others insist there are and have mass produced dictionaries to help you understand symbols that may crop up in your dreams. For example, *The Dream Encyclopedia's* compendium of dream symbols suggests that "an alien in a dream may indicate that there is difficulty adjusting to new conditions or a new environment."[1] In this, it is tempting to see a diabolical attempt to predetermine the meaning of dreams. After all, it might be argued that, if you control the symbols of dreams, you control the dreams, and, ultimately, the dreamer himself.

Where do the Messages Come From?

Scripture reveals that our thought life is impacted by three main influences — the Kingdom of Light or God, the natural man or our flesh, and the Kingdom of Darkness or Satan.

Out of the well-spring of the flesh arises "the lust of the flesh, the lust of the eyes and the pride of life" (1 Jn. 2:16). Lust and pride are powerful temptations used to attack our weak spots. Embracing temptation, even momentarily, allows Satan to penetrate the mind. Stimulation and temptation are important aspects of Satan's strategy to gain a foothold in the mind. Our environment provides the Enemy with much opportunity. Humans are fearfully and wonderfully made by the Creator with faculties that allow them to perceive stimuli originating from outside or inside the body. Each sense is a natural gateway which can be hijacked by the Enemy. Each is linked to the mind through the body's intricate wiring.

Dream researchers have discovered that external stimuli during sleep, such as "train whistles, roosters crowing, lights flashing, [and] sprays of cold water" are often incorporated into dreams. Because of this phenomenon, they have the audacity to suggest that the "army of biblical heroes may have changed the course of history not owing to angelic intervention but because they slept on their hand kind of funny."[2] We cannot deny the truth, however, that the enemy has at his disposal the full array of physical phenomena to confuse, intimidate, and deceive human beings. The

Center at its Bayview campus in Baltimore, Maryland and the Dream and Nightmare Laboratory in Montreal, Canada are just two prominent examples of how sleep and dreaming have entered the realm of academia. In fact, one catalog[4] of dream resources lists, in the United States alone, 231 academic associations, centers, clinics, and institutes which specialize in the science of dreams.

In spite of the tremendous investment into the scientific study of sleep and dreaming, little noticeable progress has been made. Harvard neurophysiologist J. Allan Hobson recently discovered neuromodulators in the brain stem that regulate mood, meaning, cognition, and emotion. While Hobson's discovery is a breakthrough in the world of science, where each building block is an important achievement, it is a minor contribution to our understanding of dreams. It does support the notion that REM sleep is essential to the process of assimilating new information,[5] but this adds nothing to the layman's understanding. From a practical point of view, little more is known today about dreaming than at the turn of the century, or indeed, from the beginning of history!

Conversely, it can not be denied that achievements in the arts and social sciences, and incredible

21

breakthroughs in science and technology have been attributed to dreams. Harriet Tubman, best known for her humanitarian work rescuing slaves fleeing the South during the Civil War era, mapped out many of the routes used by the Underground Railroad based upon details derived from dreams. Igor Stravinsky received the music for "Rite of Spring" in a dream and Billy Joel admits to using dreams to write the tunes to most of his songs, including "River of Dreams." Dreams inspired the work of Albert Einstein and Thomas Edison. In fact, Einstein credited the uniform field theory to information received in dreams.

The study of pre-cognitive or predictive dreams reveals that dreams clearly transcend time and space. Some believe that pre-cognitive dreams are evidence that the future exists in some form in the present. According to an expert in group theory, a field of mathematics that forms the foundation for quantum physics, Israeli mathematician Dr. Eliyahu Rips stated, "The Creator is not confined by time and space. For us the future is non-existent. For the Creator, the whole universe from beginning to end was seen in one stroke."[6] Einstein believed that time is multi-directional, with the future and past existing simultaneously. He once said that "the distinction between past, present, and future is only an illusion, however persistent."[7]   Indeed, Scripture tells us that God knows the end from the beginning (Is. 46:10).

Rips became known through his work on the discovery that the Hebrew Bible is actually a huge interactive database which contains the entire panorama of human events, past, present, and future. Commonly known as the "Bible code," its existence has challenged believers and non-believers alike. It has been hypothesized that the Bible code "recognizes uncertainty as part of reality"[8] and provides mankind with options which, if properly interpreted, can help it avoid catastrophe. In the same respect, perhaps pre-cognitive dreams are part of some intricately designed warning system. One must wonder how the course of world events might have been altered had more people heeded their dreams.

Napoleon dreamed about his defeat at Waterloo before it actually happened. Native Americans decided when and where to move their camps, and whether or not to make war based upon dreams. Abraham Lincoln dreamed about his assassination one full week before he was gunned down at Ford's Theater. George Patton dreamed his battle strategies before implementing them in real life on the theater of war. It is a very common

23

phenomenon for individuals to dream about an illness before the external symptoms become manifest.[9]

Omniscience and omnipotence describe the character of God, and provide for Him knowing the future. Perhaps that is why pre-cognitive and predictive dreams are almost always attributed to God. But could there be another explanation? While the probabilities posed by quantum physics do indeed provide an intellectually stimulating alternative, let me ask you to consider another possibility.

I suggest that the powers and principalities of darkness, whose existence is confirmed by Scripture, are laboring diligently, around the clock, to counterfeit God's omniscience. The scenario might look like this. A spirit in opposition to the work of the Kingdom conjures up a dream in the mind of his target which appears to be about some future event. The target wakens and finds himself moving headlong toward the predicted happening which was supposedly foretold in his sleep. In the meantime, the forces of darkness are feverishly at work behind the veil to cause the event to unfold just as it was presented to the dreamer in the night. Because of the accepted illusiveness of dreams, the enemy does not usually need a direct match. Even a reasonable facsimile will convince most people that they possess some form of extrasensory perception. Enthralled by the sense of power, the cycle is likely to continue over and over again.

There is no doubt that God indeed uses dreams, visions, and the prophetic word to move forward the Kingdom enterprise. Learning to identify His unique fingerprint is critical to the believer. In the coming chapter, we take an in-depth look at the biblical record in order to establish a sound foundation for distinguishing the genuine artifact from the satanic counterfeit.

Endnotes

1. James R. Lewis, *The Dream Encyclopedia* (Visible Ink Press: Detroit, 1995), p 272.
2. George Howe Colt, "The Power of Dreams" in *Life*, 1997, p. 42.
3. Paul D Meier, Frank B. Minirth, Frank B. Wichern, Donald E. Ratcliff. *Introduction to Psychology & Counseling*. Grand Rapids, Michigan: Baker Book House, 1991, p 241.
4. James R. Lewis, *The Dream Encyclopedia* (Visible Ink Press: Detroit, 1995).
5. George Howe Colt," The Power of Dreams" in *Life*, 1997, p. 43.
6. Michael Drosnin, *The Bible Code* (New York, NY: Simon & Schuster, 1997), p. 40.
7. Ibid., p. 31.
8. Ibid., p. 173.
9. Wendy S. Pannier, *Dream Exploration Workshop*, Perry Point Veterans Affairs Medical Center, August 28, 1997.

And it shall come to pass afterward, that I will pour out my spirit upon all flesh; and your sons and your daughters shall prophesy, your old men shall dream dreams, your young men shall see visions.

Joel 2:28

2

Dreams, Visions, and the Prophetic Word

The biblical record clearly demonstrates that dreams and visions are important vehicles which God uses to communicate to His servants. We are also told that, as the end of the age presses in on us, dreams, visions, and the prophetic word will increase dramatically (Joel 2:28; Acts 2:17). These phenomena are best understood in light of God's providential care.

Divine Providence

The essence of divine providence rests in "God's care for and guidance of His creation against all opposition."[1] God's concern for his creation is couched in the terms of deeply rooted love.

> "For I am persuaded, that neither death, nor life, nor angels, nor principalities, nor powers, nor things present, nor things to come, nor height, nor depth, nor any other creature, shall be able to separate us from the love of God, which is in Christ Jesus our Lord" (Rom. 8:38, 39).

Divine providence and the love of God are integrally connected in the Lord Jesus. Indeed, "all Christian doctrine which deserves the name Christian begins with Jesus Christ. 'He is before all things and in him all things hold together'" (Col. 1:17).[2]

The Word of God reveals that "in the beginning was the Word, and. . . All things were made by him; and without him was not any thing made that was made" (Jn. 1:1-3). The love of God is *in* Christ Jesus who himself created the universe and in whom "all things hold together." In other words, God's love holds the solar system in balance.

Once God created, creation itself became a tangible part of the equation, thereby setting the active characteristics of divine providence into motion. God began to care about what He created. Consequently, divine providence, or God's love for the objects of his creative activities, established a relationship characterized by reciprocity. His concern exacts a complementary stream of adoration which must

30

originate with the creature, flowing outward and upward to God. "According to the divine purpose of creation, human beings are intimately involved with God in God's providential care of the universe."[3] Scripture declares that dreams, visions, and the prophetic word are just a few means among many which God uses to involve humans in His care for the created order.

The discussion of creation and divine providence is linked not just with the origin of man, but also with the fall, the history of mankind since the fall, and the blessed hope for all who have embraced the Gospel about Jesus Christ. In this regard, it is not lost to the serious student that "the doctrine of Last Things [eschatology] is vitally tied to the doctrine [of creation]. Jesus said of Himself that He is the Alpha and Omega, the beginning and the end (Rev. 1:8). . . If a person can understand the origin and end of the universe, he is better equipped to live in the present in the universe."[4] A Christian certainly cannot comprehend how dreams, visions, and the prophetic word fits into the overall scheme of things without this understanding.

Divine providence also explains how our dreams and lives, in general, can be infiltrated by forces bent on disrupting our relationships with God.

> "We are fallen creatures, weak and susceptible to a multitude of social influences and dependent upon God for our moment-by-moment existence. We are also created in the image and likeness of God."[5]

While dependence on God is the critical link to the matter of divine providence, the fact that man was made in the "image of God" (Gen. 1:26) adds an important dimension to the characteristics of created beings. As God revealed Himself through Scripture over many hundreds of years, man's view of who he is in Christ was fashioned. The greatest advances in the theology of who man is took place after the events at Calvary and, to a large extent, through the witness of the Apostles. Far beyond the truth revealed prior to the life and death of the Messiah, the Pauline Epistles developed the concept of who the believer is as a created being indwelt by Christ himself.

There is an aspect of creation which moves beyond the initial event into the lives of everyone who comes to Christ. That is the possibility to be recreated. The Scriptures reveal that the individual can be "buried with [Christ] by baptism into death: that like as Christ was raised up from the dead by the glory of the Father, even so [to] walk in newness of life" (Rom. 6:4). The saga of creation is a story about the tearing down of a perfect order through disobedience; "by one man sin entered into the world, and death by sin" (Rom. 5:12). Yet, it is divine providence which allows the human race to contemplate the recreation or being "freed from sin" (Rom. 6:7), and to be equipped and empowered by God for service through the presence of the Holy Spirit.

Finally, by seeing divine providence as harmoniously working together with dreams, visions, and the prophetic word to carry forward the purpose of God, the believer faithfully embraces the reality that these capacities find their real value in the Blessed Hope. "But the day of the Lord will come as a thief in the night; in which the heavens shall pass away with a great noise, and the elements shall melt with fervent heat, the earth also and the works that therein shall be burned up" (2 Pet. 3:10). As God created, in the very beginning, so He will recreate: "Nevertheless we, according to his promise, look for a new heavens and a new earth, wherein dwelleth righteousness" (2 Pet. 3:13).

It is the reassurance of who God is, of who we are in Him, and of his care and concern for creation which gives those who place their confidence in Him the ability to live in harmony and tranquility. Jesus benediction to the recreated being is, "Peace I leave with you, my peace I give unto you; not as the world giveth, give I unto you. Let not your heart be troubled, neither let it be afraid" (Jn. 14:27).

God is omnipresent, omnipotent, and omniscient, and He puts His mind, through Christ Jesus (2 Cor. 2:16), at our disposal. Into the matrix of God's concern for us, the capacity to "see" providentially was framed.

Dreams, Visions, and the Prophetic Word

Yahweh gave us the ability to "see" supernaturally through dreams, visions, and prophecy. Although they appear in Scripture as distinct forms of communication, we recognize them as gifts with a connectedness that transcends time, space, and geopolitical boundaries. There are over 70 references to dreams in Scripture beginning with its first mention in the King James Version of the Bible "when God came to Abimelech in a dream by night" (Gen. 20:3-8).

34

By way of a word of knowledge, God warned Abimelech that he had been deceived by Abraham and, as a result, had "taken" Abraham's wife to be his own. He commanded Abimelech to return her to Abraham. Although the dreamer does not always respond with obedience when God speaks, it is the reaction He expects. Abimelech obeyed the Lord. The biblical record appears to indicate that this was a lucid dream in which the dreamer was able to vocally engage the voice of God. Interestingly, it is in this passage that the word "prophet" is mentioned for the first time (Gen 20:7).

The main distinction between dreams, visions, and prophecy from a biblical perspective, is summed up by W.E. Vines in his celebrated dictionary. While the emphasis here is on the Greek, a word study demonstrates that the Hebrew closely parallels the Greek.

DREAM, DREAMER[6]

1. ONAR is a vision in sleep, in distinction from a waking vision, Matt. 1:20; 2:12, 13, 19, 22; 27:19.

2. ENUPNION, is, lit., what appears in sleep (en, in, *hupnos*, sleep), and ordinary dream, Acts 2:17.

A vision can be constituted by anything from a single scene to a sweeping, full color panorama replete with a full cast of characters and lively dialogue.

VISION[7]

1. HORAMA, that which is seen (*horaō*), denotes (a) a spectacle, sight, Matt. 17:9; Acts 7:31 ("sight"); (b) an appearance, vision, Acts 9:10 (ver. 12 in some mss.); 10:3, 17, 19; 11:5; 12:9; 16:9, 10; 18:9.

2. HORASIS, sense of sight, is rendered "visions" in Acts 2:17; Rev. 9:17.

3. OPTASIS (alt. form of *opsis,* the act of seeing), from *optanō*, to see, a coming into view, denotes a vision in Luke 1:22,; 24:23; Acts 26:19; 2 Cor. 12:1.

In essence, a vision occurs while awake and a dream occurs during sleep. A close look at the dreams recorded in Scripture reveal them to be relatively short in duration. Visions, on the other hand, are often panoramic, filling up page after page. Perhaps the most notable example of the panorama of vision is the Revelation of Jesus Christ given to the Apostle John on the prison island called Patmos.

Alongside dreams and visions, prophecy is added. The prophetic word is the speaking forth of that which cannot be known by natural means.

PROPHECY, PROPHESY, PROPHESYING[8]

PROPHETIA signifies the speaking forth of the mind and counsel of God (*pro*, forth, *phēmi*, to speak: see PROPHET); in the N.T. it is used (*a*) of the gift, e.g., Rom. 12:6; 1 Cor. 12:10; 13:2; (*b*) either of the exercise of the gift or of that which is prophesied, e.g. Matt. 13:14; 1 Cor. 13:8; 14:6, 22 and 1 Thess. 5:20, "prophesying (s);" 1 Tim. 1:18; 4:14; 2 Pet. 1:20,21; Rev. 1:3; 11:6; 19:10; 22:7, 10, 18, 19.

'Though much of O.T. prophecy was purely predictive, see Micah 5:2, e.g., and cp. John 11:51, prophecy is not necessarily, nor even primarily, fore-telling. It is the declaration of that which cannot be known by natural means, Matt. 26:68, it is the forth-telling of the will of God, whether with reference to the past, the present, or the future, see Gen. 20:7; Deut. 18:18; Rev. 10:11; 11:3. . . .'"

The speaking forth of the mind and counsel of God does not necessarily involve dreams and visions. Prophets often prophesied under a direct unction from God.

"Then the Lord put forth his hand, and touched my mouth. And the Lord said unto me, Behold, I have put my words in thy mouth. See, I have this day set thee over the nations and over the kingdoms, to root out, and to pull down, and to destroy, and to throw down, to build, and to plant. Moreover the word of the Lord came unto me, saying. . ." (Jer. 1:9-11).

Nowhere do we find a biblical basis for the presumption that dream interpretation is a natural by-product of the prophetic ministry. Because certain prophets were used by God to interpret dreams, it should not be automatically assumed that those who interpret dreams are also prophets. Furthermore, you do not have to be a prophet to find meaning from your dreams.

Does God Speak to Unbelievers through Dreams and Visions?

Does God speak to the unbeliever through dreams, visions, and direct unction? Scripture's answer is, "Yes." He can and, from time to time, does speak to individuals who are not part of the family of God.

One of the most prominent examples in Scripture of God's use of an individual outside His chosen people is Balaam, the soothsayer of Pethor. Hired by King Balak of Moab to curse the Israelites, Balaam encountered God: "The Lord put a word in Balaam's mouth" (Num. 23:5), and instead of a curse, he spoke a blessing. To be sure, Yahweh is sovereign and He uses whom He chooses. In the record of Balaam's encounter with God, the Word tells us "the Lord [even] opened the mouth of the donkey" (Num. 22:28).

Instances of God's use of dreams and visions in the lives of those outside His chosen people, as well as the unsaved, appear to be exceptions rather than the rule, and seem to always accomplish a providential purpose. For example, the dream of Egypt's Pharaoh (Gen. 41) was used to preserve the seed of Abraham by placing Joseph in a position to be supernaturally used by God and thereby exalted to a place of stature in the Egyptian kingdom. Prophetic words given to the apostate kings of Israel, as well as the visions given to Nebuchadnezzar (Daniel 2:3, 26) and Belshazzar (Dan. 7:1) are further examples of the redemptive use of dreams.

In the New Testament age of grace, it can be argued that, while God may indeed elect to speak to the unbeliever, when this occurs, his initial calls are redemptive, leading to salvation.

Predators and the Dreamgate

Since mankind fell from grace, the forces of darkness have engaged in a relentless assault on the mind which can only be withstood in and through the power of the

Cross. As often occurs with the dream, they may sow all manner of perverse, self-deprecating, and destructive thoughts directly into the mind in order to tempt the target in an area of weakness, create animosity, evoke fear, and stimulate anxiety. This is precisely what the Apostle Paul was referring to when he described how Christians are to respond to "the fiery darts of the wicked" (Eph. 6:16).

The forces of darkness are predators, stalking their prey in order to gain a foothold. That is why the Apostle Paul admonished believers "[not to] give place to the devil" (Eph. 4:27). The concept of "gateways"[9] or footholds are important to the study of dreams because the uncrucified thought life (Gal. 2:20) represents an open invitation for a satanic attack.

Night terrors and nightmares are good examples of how dreams can be used as a vehicle for predators to strike at a target. Nightmares are generally regarded as horrible dreams that terrorize the dreamer. Often, the victim is paralyzed and not able to escape some form of attack or life threatening event.

My only real experience with a nightmare has been indelibly etched into my mind. It occurred after a terrible accident when I was ten years old. I had just returned from emergency surgery and was sleeping in

40

our downstairs den when I dreamed I was being trampled by wild horses. I awoke screaming in horror and panic.

Of course, other than the coincidental appearance of horses in my dream, the "mares" which occur in the night have nothing to do with the animals. *Mære* in Old English "denoted a sort of evil spirit or goblin which sat on sleepers' chests and gave them bad dreams."[10] Mankind's modern day sophistication does not make room for goblins or evil spirits, but to those who have experienced a nightmare, and from the Christian's perspective, the Old English had the right idea.

Dream Predators

One of the earliest lessons Christians learn is that, upon surrendering their lives to Jesus, they are thrust into a battle. On one side is God, Jesus, the Holy Spirit, and the heavenly Host. On the other side is Satan and the hordes of hell, otherwise known as dark-angels or demons. Demons are usurpers who attempt to appropriate territory that does not belong to them. They will move in to possess all that the individual does not stand against and demand as his birthright. Dreams are a powerful doorway which demons attempt

41

to use to gain control. Since demons cannot wade through the blood of Jesus which covers the believer's life, I am not necessarily referring to any form of possession. Please allow me to explain.

The term "demon possession" has caused much confusion because it implies ownership. In actuality, demons own nothing. God created everything in existence (Gen. 1:1) and owns what He creates, including demons. The issue is not one of ownership, but one of control or influence, which exist by degree, from limited to unrestricted. Some experts refer to these levels of access in terms of stages of control which include simple subjection, demonization, obsession, and possession.

A vivid example of the predatorial activities of the forces of darkness comes to us out of the occult tradition. We are informed that "nightmares come from demons — especially from the SUCCUBUS and INCUBUS, demonic creatures who attack sleeping humans sexually. The succubus is a female form, which attacks sleeping men, while the incubus is in male form, and attacks sleeping women."[11] The ultimate objective is control.

Whatever names might be given to the levels of control, they are manmade. The Bible merely

42

classifies the work of dark-angels as internal or external. Whether the control is insipid or intense and turbulent, it is still the result of the operation of demons trafficking where they do not belong. Steps must be taken to drive them back to their rightful place.

The Dreamgate

Gateways are the primary mechanisms used by the forces of darkness to penetrate a target. A gateway is a door through which demons are granted a legal right to enter the life of an individual. As I already suggested, the world of dreams represents one such door. Once "inside" the enemy attempts to establish a beachhead to launch operations. From this vantage point, the host is viciously harassed and manipulated. The presence of demons may or may not be obvious, and they will stand their ground until forced to leave.

Once a gateway is in place, a right-of-way has been granted through which inroads are built. Since many forms of the enemy's penetration are benign in appearance, countless unsuspecting people are duped into giving him ground. One of the cases I make in this book is that New Age dream enthusiasts are wittingly or unwittingly encouraging people to use techniques which appear harmless, but are actually

43

occultic methods to conjure the powers of darkness. Demons often appear as beautiful, shimmering angels of light (2 Cor. 11:14).

The Christian community must be enlightened about the devil's techniques, especially as they are used to harness the power of dreams. Once properly equipped, we will be able to resist the beguiling work of the evil one long before the battle escalates into a full-fledged struggle for the soul. It is a fallacy that once an individual has given his heart to Jesus Christ and been born again, the enemy can no longer gain a foothold in his life (Eph. 4:27). Unsealed gateways are open invitations for attack.

The scenario of a self-fulfilling prophecy painted in Chapter 1 is a perfect example of how the enemy might use the dream gateway. But let's take it one step further by demonstrating how an unsealed gateway such as "lust" might be used by the enemy. While the example which follows focuses on sexuality, we must be mindful of the fact that lusts of the flesh acted out during sleep may also include insidious dreams like those of "found money" or prestige and power. As King Solomon well understood, "a dream cometh through the multitude of business" (Eccl. 5:3).

44

A young man has been seen plotting the sexual conquest of a woman with whom he works. To the forces of darkness, his body language and suggestive speech are sure indicators that he might be an easy mark. When the fellow lays his head down on the bed, a fiery dart soars into his mind and explodes as an incredibly sensuous dream in which he finds himself in the throes of passion. Something tells him this was a pre-cognitive dream.

Across town, the woman turns off the lights and curls up in bed. She is vulnerable, having just emerged from a bad relationship. The powers of the air use their influence to titillate her senses and awaken desire in her heart for the young man. She may experience dreams about a new relationship or sudden change in living conditions, suggesting that her life is about to undergo a dramatic change.

A few days pass and, then, during a private moment which had been carefully arranged, the trap is sprung and the two are drawn together in a sexual union. The young man has his conquest. Some time later, he is reminded about the dream and is favorably impressed by the power of the dream. In reality, his new found respect is not in the dream but for the spirit forces which controlled the dream.

To those who are believers in the power of dreams, a strong note of caution must be sounded. The chapter which follows is devoted to doing that.

Endnotes

1. *New International Version Disciple's Study Bible* (Nashville, TN: Holman Bible Publishers, 1988), p. 1737.
2. David Vestal, *The Doctrine of Creation* (Nashville, TN: Broadman, 1989), p. 10.
3. Iris V. Cully and Kendig Brubaker Cully, *Encyclopedia of Religious Education* (New York, NY: Harper & Row, Publishers, 1990), p. 515.
4. David Vestal, *The Doctrine of Creation* (Nashville, TN: Broadman, 1989), p. 104.
5. Paul D. Ackerman, *In God's Image After All* (Grand Rapids, MI: Baker Book House), p. 48.
6. Ibid., "D" at p 338.
7. W.E. Vines. *Vine's Expository Dictionary of New Testament Words.* Oliphants, Ltd., 1940, "V" at p 190.
8. Ibid., "P" at p. 221.
9. For a more thorough discussion of gateways consult: J.D. Kallmyer, *The Demons Behind the New Age: And How To Defeat Them* (Havre de Grace, MD: Moriah Press, 1997).
10. John Ayto, *Dictionary of Word Origins* (New York, NY: Arcade Publishing, Inc., 1990), p. 365.
11. Charles Walker, *The Encyclopedia of the Occult* (Avenel, NJ: Random House Value Publishing, Inc., 1995), p 180.

Today the New Age movement represents what I believe is the greatest counterfeit spiritual revival the world has ever known. Satan, in a last-ditch effort as the return of Christ approaches, is attempting to imitate the tremendous explosions of evangelism and genuine Holy Spirit revival we have seen around the world over the last decade. A sort of satanic "Pentecost" of the New Age, occultic, cultic and Eastern mystical ideas is sweeping the globe.

Paul McGuire

3

Beware! Things that Go Bump in the Night

Summary of occult dream practices

If you were to develop an interest in dreams, where would you go for information? In times past, the earnest student would probably begin her quest for knowledge by going to the library or bookstore. Now, the chances are, especially if she has a computer, she will not leave home at all. Instead, she will just sit down and log onto the internet. Whether it is the local library, town bookstore, or the internet, however, the seeker will probably end up utterly bewildered by the bizarre potpourri of books and articles which stretch across the ages from the present day back into ancient times. To be sure, the interest in dreams and visions is far from a new phenomenon.

One of the wisest men who ever lived declared that "there is no new thing under the sun" (Eccl. 1:9). Inasmuch as this true, the term "New Age," which is often associated with the modern day study of dreams and visions, is truly a contradiction in terms. In the earliest days of the history of mankind, everything modern man presumptuously calls "New Age" was acknowledged as present and pervasive, and the children of God were strongly admonished to steer clear of them.

> "There shall not be found among you any one that maketh his son or his daughter to pass through the fire, or that useth divination, or an observer of times, or an enchanter, or a witch. Or a charmer, or a consulter with familiar spirits, or a wizard, or a necromancer. For all that do these things are an abomination unto the LORD: and because of these abominations the LORD thy God doth drive them out from before thee" (Deut. 18:10-12).

Historical and archaeological records reveal interest in dreams at the earliest eras of civilization. In the ancient empires of Greece, China, Egypt, and Assyria, temples were constructed and used to incubate dreams. Dream incubation is the practice of seeking dreams for a specific reason and is actually a form of occult divination.

Through the ages, dreams have been ascribed occultic significance. "Occultists have always believed that the hidden, or occult, world is far more important than the visible material world."[1] Dreams are regarded as a key to unlock the secret realms. While the occult is alive and thriving, the "discoveries" of psychoanalysis, however, have raised a significant challenge to the traditional occultic beliefs about dreams.

Sigmund Freud, Dreamwork, and Psychoanalysis

The modern, scientific interest in dream exploration began with Austrian psychoanalyst Sigmund Freud (1856-1939). In 1913, the 500-page *The Interpretation of Dreams* was published by The MacMillan Company. Freud made a statement then which remains true today.

> "To write a history of our scientific knowledge of dream problems is so difficult because, however valuable some parts of this knowledge may have been, no progress in definite directions has been discernible."[2]

Freud's work on dreams is still considered a masterpiece, but is laborious reading for most, and has little impact to the student of dreams except to demonstrate where the academic interest in dreams began and how it has evolved.

Freud saw the subconscious as an unilluminated part of the mind that possesses incredible power to mold thoughts, feelings, and actions. Other researchers explain that Freud is simply repackaging a division of our mental existence that has been identified and described over the ages using terms such as "super-ego, the inner power, the super-consciousness, the unconscious, the subconscious, and various other names."[3] The ancients called it "the spirit" and New Agers call it the "Universal Mind."

> "No matter what we call it. . . it is recognized as the essence of life, and the limits of its power are unknown. It never sleeps. It comes to our support in times of great trouble, it warns us of impending danger, often aids us to do that which seems impossible. It guides us in many ways and when properly employed performs so-called miracles."[4]

Freud developed two concepts which comprised dreamwork, the subconscious process which he believed repackages dream images that could be distressing. The narrative account of the dream, as it actually occurred and could be recounted the following morning by the dreamer, is called the *manifest dream*. The actual, hidden meaning forms the content of the *latent dream*. In dreamwork, the latent dream is censored through five main subconscious processes: displacement, condensation, symbolization, projection, and secondary revision. According to Freud, censorship occurs because the dreamer has fantasies that can only be acted out through the privacy of dreams because to do so during the waking hours would violate accepted standards of behavior.

Freud's work on dreams, coupled with his psychoanalytical techniques, have deeply influenced modern dream interpretation. "The general view nowadays is that while dreams do relate in many instances to the future of the dreamer, they must be interpreted with the aid of a psychological key relevant to that dreamer."[5] This belief promotes the idea that fixed methods for interpreting dreams and their symbols are not valid. Those involved in the New Age Movement would tend to strongly disagree.

The New Age Movement
and the Merchandising of Dreams

What is really appealing to contemporary dream enthusiasts are the dozens of trendy new kinds of dream-related merchandise that are on the market. Among them are: dream encyclopedias or alphabetized lists of symbols that crop up in dreams along with their meanings; methodologies which teach dreamers how to use visualization, meditation, crystals, and vitamins to access past lives or solve problems; dream pillows that contain aromatic herbs to induce sleep and heighten dreams; and dream packs which contains everything needed to inspire, control, interpret, and record dreams.

Christians should be cautioned against using these kinds of products for a number of extremely important reasons. Nowhere in Scripture do dreamers use herbs, meditation, crystals, vitamins, or any other aid to control dreams. While dream pillows may enhance a dreamer's ability to hear from dark-angels, God needs no such medium to speak and be heard. In fact, Joseph's pillows were rocks, and he had no problem hearing from God!

"And he lighted upon a certain place, and tarried there all night, because the sun was set; and he took of the stones of that

54

place, and put them for his pillows, and lay down in that place to sleep" (Gen. 28:11).

Any means or methods used to manipulate, enhance, or control dreams are simply other forms of occult divination. Furthermore, believers must look beyond the artifacts themselves to the inventors and authors. Almost without exception, you will find dream products manufactured and marketed by individuals who are connected in some way to the New Age Movement.

The New Age is also "called the 'Great Dispensation,' the 'Age of Understanding'" and as one prophet declared is "the end of the world as we know it."[6] Prominent Christian scholars now view the New Age as "a kind of ecumenical movement of Eastern, occult and New Consciousness groups [which] network together."[7] As such, the Movement is a diffusely organized group of people who have picked up the New Age and have purposed themselves toward the generalized common goal of spreading the philosophies associated with it. "The massive 'New Age Movement' presents a potpourri of teachings, some of which sound Christian. Many of them are presented under the guise of being scientific and medical when in reality they are simply Hindu practices."[8]

"New Agers refer to their belief system as 'The Plan' and woe to anyone who does not agree with them."[9] Christians are enemies of humanity who will be destroyed, according to New Ager Alice Bailey. "The world problem is essentially a religious problem and behind all strife in every department of world thought today is to be found the religious element."[10]

Albeit not openly, and under the guise of more acceptable names, New Age dream quest gurus encourage their adherents to use divinatory arts to expand and exploit their dream potential. Among them are *prophetia* or channeling the influx of a spirit or disincarnate entity to receive supernatural power and *pyramidum scientia*, divination through mathematical, geometrical, and spiritual connections between archetypes and earthly counterparts.[11]

Other forms of divination include seeking the answers to questions by summoning spirit creatures by using the Ouija board, foretelling the future using tarot cards, and simple fortune telling. Practices utilizing the rod and pendulum, water witching, psychometry, predicting dreams and visions, and crystal balls all represent extremely hazardous forms of occult divination which invite conversation with the demonic. The connection between the occult and dreams is clear in Scripture. King Nebuchadnezzar called forth his "magicians, and the astrologers, and the sorcerers" (Daniel 2:2) to interpret his dreams.

Engaging in any activity that could be construed as occultic is extremely dangerous because it swings the gate wide open to demonic influences. Among the practices which should be repudiated by Christians are divination, magic and spiritism, or any combination of them.

Although the basic messages may vary in the way they are presented, there are a number of common threads which, when flushed out, provide the basic doctrine of the New Age Movement. Three overarching tenets bind the major segments of the New Age Movement together: all is one, the key to divine illumination is within, and deification of self. *A Key*

Monism or the "all is one" doctrine is perhaps the most significant tenet of the New Age Movement. New Age guru Shirley MacLaine says that, "Everything it is, everything we are, everything we do, is linked to everything else. There is no separateness."[12] "New Agers argue that since 'all is one' and the universe is eternal — you are eternal."[13]

Second, according to the New Age Movement, the key to unlocking the mysteries of the universe lies within each individual's consciousness. Hence, one must journey into the "inner child" if he hopes to find the key. Dreams can be a dynamic medium to accomplish this. "New Agers [turn] to Eastern gurus, channels (alleged disembodied spirits which are said to speak from another dimension), extraterrestrials, dolphins, crystals, [as well as] the 'Higher Self' within."[14] Meditation is often used in conjunction with reaching the dream state to achieve "self-realization" or attain "higher consciousness." Medical doctor Rebecca Brown warns tinkerers.

> "'Self-realization' is actually the process whereby a person learns to control his spirit. 'Higher consciousness' is achieved as a person begins to communicate with the various demon spirits. Often, people have a particular demon whom they call their 'guide,' or 'counselor.'"[15]

New Agers, of course, would deny this. There appears to be an obliviousness among practitioners to malevolent spirits masquerading as angels of light. Like the Gnostics of the New Testament era, good and evil to them are viewed as emanations which come from the same source. "[Man] is the totality of all that The Father is: God Supreme."[16] In fact, "there is no difference between creature and creator as both are

58

one."[17] Each individual, New Agers claim, possesses the key to divine illumination. Look inward and you tap into that energy source. From this perspective, dreams become just another medium through which the enchanted dreamer can discover the universe within himself.

> "Sleep is the great mother who feeds our spirits and untangles the threads of our daily lives so that we can wake to weave a new day."[18]

Yes, sleep can be a "great mother" feeding our spirits, but, entered this way, it becomes a dynamic gateway used by forces of darkness to penetrate the human , psyche and the "great mother" is no other than the Prince of Darkness himself, Lucifer, the Light-bearer.

Edgar Cayce: A Father
of the New Age Movement

Edgar Cayce (1877-1945), a southern Presbyterian Sunday School teacher, is called "a prophet of the New Age. . . He said he would return in 1998 as a world liberator if he so desired, to help bring about the New Age."[19]   Whatever humility this would-be Messiah possessed at the beginning of his road to fame certainly became distorted over time.

I will never forget the image of Edgar Cayce's name the first time I really paid any attention to it. I was riding a Mass Transit Administration bus to work one bright morning. The bus stopped at one of its usual corners and a young, nice looking woman dressed in black boarded. I recall thinking that she looked like a witch. She sat in the seat right in front of me and proceeded to pull out a book to read to pass the time. Across the cover was the name Edgar Cayce in big black letters. My eyes were next drawn to a ring on the woman's left hand which bore the satanic pentagram. After doing some research about Cayce, I was not the least bit surprised that a satanist might be interested in his unusual powers.

Cayce is probably the most renowned figure in the field of dreams and dream interpretation. While it is reported that Cayce, in the early years, refused to profit from his "gift," since his death, his progeny have turned his life into a multi-million dollar industry. The cornice of the empire is the non-profit Cayce Foundation headquartered in Virginia Beach, Virginia. The way the Foundation bills its namesake should, in itself, alarm even the most naive Christian.

"America's most famous clairvoyant reveals the secrets of the paranormal world — and shows you how to use them to achieve a happier life."[20]

Cayce, born in Hopkinsville, Kentucky had a gift that continues to bring him international renown. While he has been touted to be a devout Christian — "children admired him as a warm and friendly Sunday School teacher"[21] — the simple fact alone that he was able to see and talk to relatives who had recently died thrusts him into a category of persons to be avoided.

According to a biography, Cayce gave "readings" which, by his death, numbered over 14,000. People who knew him say that he was able "to put his own unconscious mind in complete communication with the minds of others,"[22] an ability called telepathy. It is said that he could receive a dream at night and then "later put himself to sleep and ask for and receive, an interpretation of what he had dreamed."[23] The same was true, say his biographers, of visions he would receive. After entering into a trance, Cayce would begin to make observations which appeared as if he was actually in another location. This practice is a common practice among New Agers called channelling. Cayce admitted to "receiving contact from 'some benevolent spirit or physician from the other side.'"[24]   He was also a firm believer in reincarnation.

The thing that really bewilders the wide-eyed novice is that the fruit of Cayce's readings appear to be good, wholesome, and, at first blush, even Christ-like. Countless people were remarkably healed of illnesses. The life and work of Cayce is a strong reminder that even "good" works, apart from Christ, amount to nothing.   Cayce represents the pseudo-Christian dabbler in the occult who, realizing a gift, misinterprets it as being from God and pursues it with all out gusto.

Cayce's greatest accomplishment is not anything he may have done in his lifetime. It is, on the other hand, the international monument to his life which has been erected in his honor at his death. The books, tapes, and videos published by the Cayce Foundation and the seminars conducted by its subsidiary, the Association for Research and Enlightenment, have made believers out of millions of people that contact with benevolent spirits is not only possible, but desirable and wholesome. Of course, we know that these are really malevolent dark-angels masquerading as angels of light.

Note:

＊ occult

Key

Archetypes, Folklore, and
Joseph Campbell

An inquiry into dreams is not complete without a serious look at archetypes, constant images, or universal dream symbols. Which term is used depends on who is discussing the subject. The philosophical and sociological basis for the existence of archetypes rests in the New Age belief that there is a collective conscious which reveals itself through mythology and folklore. This is the way Swiss psychotherapist Carl Jung (1875-1961) understood dreams. His ideas are best known to the dream weaver through the work of scholar Joseph Campbell (1904-1987) who promoted the concept of the "sacred story."

> "For example, a constant image is that of the conflict of the eagle and serpent. The serpent bound to the earth, the eagle in spiritual flight — isn't that something we all experience? And then, when the two amalgamate, we get a wonderful dragon, a serpent with wings. All over the earth people recognize these images. Whether I'm reading Polynesian or Iroquois or Egyptian myths, the images are the same, and they are talking about the same problems."[25]

Campbell believed that "the myth is the public dream and the dream is the private myth."[26] People, he says, become neurotic when there is dissonance between the private myth and the public dream. The theory is extended to promote the idea that understanding the symbols or constant images of mythology is essential to interpreting dreams. As a result, dream dictionaries have emerged to be one of the most popular tools in the New Age arsenal. These are books that define the symbols of dreams in more or less universal application. As I have already suggested, it is not difficult to see the work of a diabolical force guiding the pen of New Age dream weavers in an attempt to control the dream, the symbols of dream, and the dreamer himself.

For those who are acquainted with the New Age Movement, the following statement by Campbell will sound familiar: "All the gods, all the heavens, all the worlds, are within us. They are magnified dreams."[27] Campbell became a pop phenomenon before he died. His influence reverberates throughout the New Age Movement and has been embedded into the fabric of New Age dream weavers.

Nowhere in my review of the vast New Age compendium of fact, theory, speculation, and fiction is the attitude of adherents about Jesus Christ more clearly reflected than in the work by Campbell.

"One thing that comes out in myths, for example, is that at the bottom of the abyss comes the voice of salvation. . . identifying the Christ in you. The Christ in you doesn't die. The Christ in you survives death and resurrects. Or you can identify that with Shiva."[28]

At the basis of the New Age belief in archetypes is the assertion that Jesus Christ is just another manifestation of a common myth, an allusion that should cause Christians to automatically reject Campbell and the mythology of dreams he and his followers promote.

Dreams, Sorcery, and Carlos Castenada

When I was a teenager, my circle of friends were immersed in the drug culture. On one level, drug use was about money and thrill seeking. On another level, however, there was an earnest and purposeful attempt to use peyote, LSD, and mescaline to harness the supernatural. It was widely believed, and confirmed by mystics, that drugs were a powerful tool to open doors to the supernatural. The work of Carlos Castenada guided our pursuit.

Castenada skyrocketed onto the public stage with the publication of the first in a series of books entitled

The Teachings of Don Juan: A Yaqui Way of Knowledge. His books about Don Juan, a Yaqui shaman, have since moved out of the 60's hippie movement into the New Age mainstream and are powerful reinforcements to the notion that dreams have enormous psychic potential.

Don Juan taught Castenada, an anthropologist by profession, how to use the techniques of astral projection, sorcery, lucid dreaming, and natural hallucinogens to interrupt "the plausibility structure of ordinary reality."[29]

Don Juan taught that at the mid-point of the body is the "assemblage point,"[30] the true center of energy. Perception is the product of selecting and aligning emanations — energy fields which give rise to the images we see in the real world. According to the sorcerer, the assemblage point shifts in dreaming. If not handled correctly, the outcome can be dangerous. Dreams have inconceivable power which can be harnessed by learning the art of manipulating the dream body, which comes into existence when the assemblage point moves. Controlling the dream body is simply another term for channeling or astral projection.

By bringing the name Castenada into the discussion of dreams, we add drugs and sorcery to the relationship between the New Age movement and the techniques it promotes to harness the power of dreams.

Dream Incubation

The ancient Greeks gave the concept of incubation its start with the construction of hundreds of temples dedicated to the God Asclepius. According to Greek mythology,[31] Asclepius was the mortal son of Coronis of Thessaly, one of Apollo's lovers. She was executed for unfaithfulness, but Asclepius was rescued by Zeus while still in the womb as the body of Coronis burned on the funeral pyre. He was then placed in the care of the centaur Chiron who taught him the healing arts using "herbs and gentle incantations and cooling potions."[32] When Asclepius dared to raise a man from the dead for a large fee, he too was executed by Zeus. No mortal would be allowed to possess such power. "For hundreds of years after his death the sick and maimed and the blind came for healing to his temples. There they would pray and sacrifice, and after that go to sleep. Then in their dreams the good physicians would reveal to them how they could be cured."[33]

Like the Greeks, New Age dream weavers paint dream incubation as a harmless way to harness dream power to achieve specific results, which includes healing. In the methodologies published, people are encouraged to establish "communication" with the dream itself. Nowhere is Yahweh, Jesus Christ, and the Holy Spirit mentioned, except to say that some people "think" they get their dreams from God.

Similar in many ways to incubation is "dream catching." Drawn from the shamanistic practices of Native Americans, it is believed that dreams can be caught by elaborate contraptions made out of objects taken from the occult repertoire and suspended above the head of the dreamer. The goal of dream catching, as well as dream incubation, is to be able to create a dream-on-demand environment in which the dreamer can divine a dream that is very clear and understandable, and responds to his or her specific needs and desires.[34] This is nothing more than occult divination.

Note

In this chapter, we took a brief look at the devices Christians are admonished to avoid completely in their quest to know and understand the meaning of dreams, visions, and the prophetic word. In the next chapter,

68

we take an in-depth look at the right way to go about hearing the voice of God.

Endnotes

1. Charles Walker, *The Encyclopedia of the Occult* (Avenel, NJ: Random House Value Publishing, Inc., 1995), p. 30.
2. Sigmund Freud, *The Interpretation of Dreams* (New York, NY: The MacMillan Company, 1913), p. 3.
3. Claude M. Bristol, *The Magic of Believing* (New York, NY: Simon & Shuster, 1948), p. 36.
4. Ibid.
5. Charles Walker, *The Encyclopedia of the Occult* (Avenel, NJ: Random House Value Publishing, Inc., 1995), p. 180.
6. Mary Ellen Carter, *Edgar Cayce on Prophecy* (New York, NY: Paperback Library, Inc., 1968), p. 10.
7. Gordon R. Lewis, "Foreward" in Douglas R. Groothuis, *Unmasking the New Age* (Downers Grove, IL: Intervarsity Press, 1986), p. 9.
8. Rebecca Brown, *Prepare for War* (Springdale, PA.: Whitaker House, 1987), p. 185.
9. Ibid., p. 200.
10. Douglas R. Groothuis, *Unmasking the New Age* (Downer's Grove, IL: Intervarsity Press, 1986), pp. 119-120, 127.
11. Charles Walker, *The Encyclopedia of the Occult* (Avenel, NJ: Random House Value Publishing, 1995), pp. 175-176.
12. Shirley MacLaine, *Going Within* (New York, NY: Bantam Books, 1989), p. 85.
13. Brad T. Bromling, "Satan's 'New Age' Approach" in *Reason & Revelation*, (Montgomery, AL: Apologetics Press, Inc., October 1989), p. 37
14. Ibid., p. 38.

15. Rebecca Brown, *Prepare for War* (Springdale, PA.: Whitaker House, 1987), p. 124.
16. J.Z. Knight (Ramtha), *Voyage to the New World: An Adventure into Unlimitedness* (New York, NY: Ballantine, 1986), p. 22.
17. Rebecca Brown, *Prepare for War* (Springdale, PA.: Whitaker House, 1987), p. 185.
18. Lynne Blackman and Kathy Corey, *A Place to Dream* (New York, NY: Warner Books, 1997).
19. Mary Ellen Carter, *Edgar Cayce on Prophecy* (New York, NY: Paperback Library, Inc., 1968), pp. 10-12.
20. Doris Agee and Hugh Lynn Cayce. *Edgar Cayce on ESP* (New York, NY: Warner Books, Inc., 1969), cover.
21. Ibid., p. 7.
22. Ibid., p. 13.
23. Ibid.
24. Ibid., pp. 40-41.
25. Joseph Campbell with Bill Moyers, *The Power of Myth* (New York, NY: Doubleday, 1988), pp. 37-18.
26. Ibid., p. 40.
27. Ibid., p. 39.
28. Ibid.
29. James R. Lewis, *The Dream Encyclopedia* (Detroit, MI: Visible Ink Press, 1995), p. 41.
30. Carlos Castenada, *The Fire From Within* (New York, NY: Simon & Schuster, Inc., 1984), pp. 106-125, 167-182.
31. Edith Hamilton, *Mythology* (Boston, MA: Little, Brown and Company, 1942), pp. 413-415.
32. Ibid., p. 414.
33. Ibid., p. 415.
34. Denise Linn. The *Hidden Power of Dreams* (New York, NY: Ballantine Books, 1988), pp. 84-85.

When we speak of what God has prepared for his people, we cannot use the language of sight. We must use the language of vision.

Willem VanGemeren

4

Facilitating and Interpreting Dreams

The right way!

If we accept the fact that there are three sources for dreams — God, Satan, and the flesh — how can you tell if a dream is from God, the enemy, or simply the rumblings of the subconscious mind? Even when you figure that out, it goes without saying that the dream has many possible interpretations. While the meaning of some dreams may be obvious, others are not. It makes all the difference in the world which means and methods you choose to interpret your dreams and whom you go to for advice and counsel.

We recognize that for everything spiritual that is birthed by God, there is a satanic counterfeit. What God uses, Satan abuses. What God protects, the enemy attempts to penetrate.. If the enemy is unable to hijack the dream itself, he will seek to infiltrate the interpretation.

How many believers would think of consulting a medium or spiritist to find out why a departed loved one turned up in a dream dazed and troubled? What earnest Christian would call the psychic hotline or go to a fortuneteller to confirm what a dream might have revealed about the future? No disciple of Christ in their right mind would bring a Ouija board or seance, or invite any occultic influence into their home? Yet, because the margins are so blurred, dreamers often naively summon occult influences into their lives in an attempt to interpret their dreams.

Unfortunately, there is not a wealth of information about the subject of dream interpretation that is written from a purely Christian perspective. Equally unfortunate is the fact that an information void seldom prevents seekers from trekking into uncharted and forbidden territory to find answers to their questions. Even when an individual is determined to avoid pagan influences, he may unwittingly be lured toward them. What would you think of the internet website which bills itself this way?

"Dreams & Visions interpreted through anointed Prophetess. Each dream is prayed over, and interpretation is given through

Holy Spirit gifts. No symbol or dream dictionaries used. Have over 150 letters of testimony regarding accuracy of interpretations. Interpretations are free."[1]

How many hundreds of well meaning believers have fallen into this web not knowing anything about nor taking the time to check into the credentials of this so-called prophetess?

The Framework

My understanding of dreams begins from the belief that God is interested in every aspect of our life. The concept of divine providence, developed in Chapter 2 of this book, provides the framework I have constructed for facilitating and interpreting dreams. Whether a dream emanates directly from God, from the flesh — our soulish conscious or subconscious minds — or is a fiery dart from the enemy, God's power to solve or resolve the mystery is at our disposal.

Our source for dream interpretation must be God. *key* In every instance in Scripture where a dream was interpreted by one of God's servants, the interpretation came quickly and with divine clarity. There was no struggle over the meaning of dream symbols or any reference to archetypes.

The connection between dreams and visions to prophecy is another matter entirely. What makes a dream prophetic. Can pre-cognitive dreams not be divinely inspired?

Varieties of Dreams

A close look at dreams and visions in the Bible reveals that there are four more or less basic kinds of divinely inspired dreams: *prima facie*, symbolic, pre-cognitive, and predictive. These are my own devices for distinguishing dream content by form.

The Prima Facie Dream. In the *prima facie* dream, there is no need for interpretation. The dream means what it says and says what it means. On a number of occasions in Scripture, an individual received a dream which provided information or direction in a manner that was unambiguous.

> "But while he thought on these things, behold, the angel of the Lord appeared unto him in a dream, saying 'Joseph, thou son of David, fear not to take unto thee Mary thy wife: for that which is conceived in her is of the Holy Ghost'" (Matt. 1:20).

The Symbolic Dream. When dreams contain symbols not readily apparent to the dreamer, he must then engage in an interpretive process in order to comprehend the meaning. A symbolic dream may or may not be predictive in character. With the involvement of God, the dream symbols may be given immediate significance.

> "Forasmuch as thou sawest that the stone was cut out of the mountain without hands, and that it brake in pieces the iron, the brass, the clay, the silver, and the gold; the great God hath made known to the king what shall come to pass hereafter: and the dream is certain, and the interpretation thereof sure" (Dan. 2:45).

The Pre-Cognitive Dream. The pre-cognitive dream occurs when an individual experiences an event in a dream or vision before it actually occurs. Symbols may be used, as in the case of Joseph when he dreamed that "the sun and the moon and the eleven stars made obeisance" to him (Gen. 37:9).

The Predictive Dream. A dream or vision which is purely predictive does not involve the dreamer himself, is about an event or series of events yet to occur, and may or may not involve symbols. The dream Daniel revealed to Nebuchadnezzar was rich with symbolism and was divinely inspired to make known "what shall be in the latter days" (Dan. 2:28).

77

On the island of Patmos, the Apostle John witnessed a series of visions about events that were yet to happen which represent a mixture of symbols and *prima facie* representations.

Dream Symbols and Scripture

Earnest students of Scripture must be careful in their treatment of dream symbols. This fact is clearly exemplified by the disagreement in Christian circles over how to interpret the Bible book of Revelation. Some people say that the incredible looking, multi-headed beasts exist exactly as John portrayed them. Others believe that John was seeing far into the future and, as a scribe, was using the language of his day to describe events which involve gadgets which had not yet been invented. One of the most prominent Christian writers who bases his interpretations on this belief is Hal Lindsey, the prominent author of the *Late Great Planet Earth.*

> "I personally tend to think that God might utilize in his judgments some modern devices of man which the Apostle John was at a loss for words to describe nineteen centuries ago! In the case just mentioned, the locusts might symbolize an advanced kind of helicopter."[2]

78

The problem with this kind of approach is that, absent a direct word from God, our interpretations might be filled with wild speculation.

The Interpretive Process

"When Joseph came to them in the morning, he saw that they were distraught. He asked Pharaoh's courtiers, who were with him in custody in his master's house, saying, 'Why do you appear downcast today?' And they said to him, 'We had dreams, and there is no one to interpret them.' So Joseph said to them, 'Surely God can interpret them! Tell me [your dreams]'" (Gen. 40:7-8).

Set forth in the following pages is a method for interpreting dreams which relies entirely on the Holy Spirit. At this junction, several important points must be underscored. While I in no way limit the power of God to help us answer questions about our lives, regardless of the source, the interpretive process which follows primarily concerns dreams and visions which originate in the mind of God. Furthermore, because our reliance is on the Holy Spirit and the gifts He gives, anybody who might attempt to test the process in a real life situation must seek counsel from mature individuals who know and understand them. I cannot emphasize enough the significance of putting to practice the biblical principle that, "Where no counsel is, the people fall: but in the multitude of counsellors there is safety" (Prov. 11:14). With relation to dreams, visions, and the prophetic word, the practical implementation of this proverb will unlikely be successful outside a body of believers who take the gifts of the Holy Spirit seriously.

Believers seeking to hear from God should rely solely on the Holy Spirit. Completely avoid the techniques suggested by New Age dream weavers to induce sleep and invoke dreams. Use of aroma therapy, dream pillows, runes, and the like, are all methods to awaken dream spirits which open gateways for penetration by the demonic. The Scripture puts no stock in special sleep positions, music to awaken the soul, or other dream paraphernalia. God spoke to those He elected, and, apart from the pagans he used as part of a greater plan, the common prerequisite was a lifestyle of yieldedness to the things of God. This means that we must ardently renew our minds daily by filling ourselves up with the Word.

"And be not conformed to this world: but be ye transformed by the renewing of your mind, that ye may prove what is the good, and acceptable, and perfect, will of God" (Rom. 12:2).

80

By letting the Spirit of the Lord fill us with His presence and power, we are able to take on the mind of Christ (1 Cor. 2:16). It is walking in our relationship with Christ that permits us to remove the influence of the prince of the power of the air from the world of dreams.

> "Wherein in time past ye walked according to the course of this world, according to the prince of the power of the air, the spirit that now worketh in the children of disobedience: Among whom also we all had our conversation in times past in the lusts of our flesh, fulfilling the desires of the flesh and of the mind; and were by nature the children of wrath, even as others. . . For through him we both have access by one Spirit unto the Father" (Eph. 2:2-3, 18).

While God informed us that in the last days "your sons and your daughters shall prophesy, your old men shall dream dreams, your young men shall see visions" (Joel 2:28), He also said that "in the latter times some shall depart from the faith, giving heed to seducing spirits, and doctrines of devils" (1 Tim. 4:1). The mind must be protected, and nurtured in the wisdom, admonition, and understanding in the Lord.

Note

81

"You will remember that the location where Jesus was crucified was called 'Golgotha,' which meant 'place of the skull.' If we will be effective in spiritual warfare, the first field of conflict where we must learn warfare is the battleground of the mind; i.e., the 'place of the skull.' For the territory of the uncrucified thought-life is the beachhead of satanic assault in our lives. To defeat the devil, we must be crucified in the place of the skull. We must be renewed in the spirit of our minds."[3]

The Lord has thoroughly equipped us to win the war t providing a full arsenal of offensive and defensi' weaponry. When the Christian puts "on the armor God [he is] really putting on Christ (Rom. 13:12-14) and putting on Christ is the best protection the beliey has to combat the wiles of the Devil. The helmet salvation, for example, affirms that our position is o of Christ's redeemed. Satan really has no dominion authority. Let me give you an example.

One young man who, after escaping out involvement in the underworld of drugs at rededicating his life to the Lord, began to experien nightmares. In his late twenties, he found himse having repetitive dreams in which he was being chase and shot at. More than once, he awoke after dreamin that he had murdered someone. It often took severa moments before he realized he was dreaming and was

82

able to shake the horror out of his consciousness. The dreams were terrifying and tormenting, and succeeded in keeping the fellow from being able to sever his present from his past to walk in the fulness of Christ. These dreams were clearly the diabolical work of the Kingdom of Darkness. The antidote came in the form of him vigilantly taking the advice of a trusted friend to renew his mind daily through prayer, meditating on the Word of God, and reading Scripture immediately before going to bed.

There are a number of things that will negatively impact sleep and interfere with the Christ-centered meditative process which the believer should take into account: extremes in temperature; medication, alcohol, street drugs, and coffee; exhaustion from too much work, not enough sleep, and strenuous physical exercise too close to bedtime.

Set forth below is a 3-step process which I believe will, if pursued with Christ-centered diligence, enable you to decipher the meaning of your dreams.

Step 1: A Life Grounded in the Lord

The believer must be adamant about living a lifestyle pleasing to the Lord. The Apostle Paul admonished believers to be clothed daily with the full armor of God (Eph. 6:13) — a literal putting on the helmet of salvation, the breastplate of righteousness, the belt of truth, the shoes of peace, and the sword of the spirit. A careless walk with the Lord will open the Christ-follower's life up to the enemy's deception and the sting of fiery darts.

> "[Be] rooted and built up in him, and stablished in the faith, as ye have been taught, abounding therein with thanksgiving. Beware lest any man spoil you through philosophy and vain deceit, after the tradition of men, after the rudiments of the world, and not after Christ" (Col. 2:7-8).

Pray without ceasing and read the Word with diligence, and live connected to a body of believers (Heb.10:25).

Step 2: Record the Dream

Keep a dream journal. Some of the most powerful dreams occur as a lucid dream or that state of being aware, during the dream, that you are dreaming. Write as much of the dream down as you can.

One of the most important factors in being able to correctly analyze and interpret dreams is accurately recording the details. It helps to have a night light, a pen, and a pad of paper near the bed. The closer you are to the dream, the more detail you will be able to remember. The farther away from the event a person gets, the less reliable the dream record will be. As much as 90% of the dream will be lost if not recorded within five minutes.

The recordkeeping process should not just include the events which transpired, but should also record colors and textures, the kinds of clothes people wore, moods, and the weather, for example. Every detail that can be remembered, no matter how insignificant, should be written down.

How do you know if a dream is worth noting? While it may seem a simplistic answer, my response is simply this: you will know. Scripture reveals that the dreamer will immediately ascertain upon waking that he has had a meaningful dream.

"When Joseph came to them in the morning, he saw that they were distraught. He asked Pharaoh's courtiers, who were with him in custody in his master's house, saying, 'Why do you appear downcast today?' And they said to him, 'We had dreams'" (Gen. 40:7-8).

"Then Pharaoh woke up; it had been a dream. In the morning his mind was troubled, so he sent for all the magicians and wise men of Egypt. Pharaoh told them his dreams, but no one could interpret them for him." (Gen. 41:7b-8).

"So [Nebuchadnezzar] summoned the magicians, enchanters, sorcerers and astrologers to tell him what he had dreamed. When they came in and stood before the king, he said to them, "I have had a dream that troubles me and I want to know what it means" (Dan. 2:2-3).

It is commonly believed that only the dreamer himself can interpret his own dream. Scripture, however, indicates there are God-inspired helpers who can assist. But, in all cases where a dream was interpreted, the interpretation bore witness with the dreamer himself. Pharaoh immediately ascertained Joseph's interpretation to be valid, as did Nebuchadnezzar when Daniel revealed the secret of his night vision. Fortunately, we know the end of the story. Both Pharaoh's and Nebuchadnezzar's dreams were used mightily of the Lord as part of His providential plan for the children of God.

When we awaken knowing that we have dreamed, but the details are sketchy, there is a high degree of likelihood that the dream emanated from flesh — the soulish subconscious mind. That is not to say that it does not have meaning and should not be taken into account. Secular research which supports the notion that dreams indeed help resolve conflict is compelling.

Nevertheless, the dreamer's first inclination should be to take the dream and it's content to the Lord.

Step 3: Submit the Dream to the Lord

After recording the dream, involve the Lord in the interpretive process from the very beginning by praying about the dream. Ask Him for the interpretation. If you have a trusted friend, pray together with that individual. Be sure that he too is rooted and grounded in the Lord. The interpretation will come. Be patient.

A significant illustration of this point is provided to us in Scripture.

"[Peter] fell into a trance, And saw heaven opened, and a certain vessel descending unto him, as it had been a great sheet knit at the four corners, and let down to the earth: Wherein were all manner of fourfooted beasts of the earth, and wild beasts, and creeping things, and fowls of the air. And there came a voice to him, Rise, Peter; kill, and eat. But Peter said, Not so, Lord; for I have never eaten any thing that is common or unclean. And the voice spake unto him again the second time, What God hath cleansed, that call not thou common. This was done thrice: and the vessel was received up again into heaven. Now while Peter doubted in himself what this vision which he had seen should mean" (Acts 10:10-17).

If someone of Peter's stature would have doubts about a dream's meaning, then we find ourselves in good company when we question the things we see in a vision. Did Peter have a method of interpretation? Not really. The Word of God simply tells us that, "While Peter thought on the vision, the Spirit [spoke]" (Acts 10:19). The meaning of the dream was given to him by the Holy Spirit, the same person we must go to for insight. The Spirit's response was not a direct revelation of facts, but was a call to action. Peter responded and quickly learned that the dream's intent was to convey to him God's will for the Gospel to be carried to "the Gentiles [upon whom] also was poured out the gift of the Holy Ghost" (Acts 10:45).

When we approach the Lord for the meaning of a dream, and when an answer seems to come, be sure to line the interpretation up with Scripture before accepting it as a final word on the matter. God's answer will always be doctrinally sound. For example, what if a person who is deceased turns up on the dream stage and makes the following statement? "Everything will be okay. You can go on now." Obviously, the Word of God prevents us from believing that the individual actually crossed the great chasm and literally appeared in the dream. There must be another explanation.

The Theology of Dream Interpretation

Jesus told us that He would not leave us alone, He promised to send us another, just like himself (Jn. 14:5-16). The Spirit itself is poured out on all flesh and it is that empowerment which enables us to live on a spiritual plane. It is my belief that dreams are primarily a spiritual phenomena and that it is understanding the activity and operation of the Spirit that enables the believer to contend effectively with them.

Conveying the idea that dreams are something to "contend" with is perhaps my highest calling in writing and publishing this book. I utterly reject the idea promoted by New Age dream weavers that you can "trust any information that is revealed."[5] Scripture clearly informs us that we battle with the flesh within ourselves and war in the heavenlies with the power and principalities of darkness. Even the most yielded Christian must admit that distinguishing the voice of God amidst the background noise of life in an embattled and embittered world is not easy. The language of dreams is no exception.

Recognizing the reality that the challenge to "contend for the faith" (Jude 1:3) exists on all fronts of

89

our mortal existence should cause us to embrace caution when it comes to dreams and dream interpretation. Fortunately, the Lord Jesus Christ gave us the most powerful weapon against deception an individual could ever hope to possess — the Holy Spirit. It is impossible to discern the divine character of dreams and visions, and what God might be saying through them, without a proper understanding of the Holy Spirit and His work in and through the Body of Christ.

The Gifts of the Holy Spirit

Harold Horton, in his masterpiece, *The Gifts of the Spirit*, declared that Yahweh has divided His omnipotence and omniscience "into nine more or less equal parts for distribution"[6] to the Saints.

> "Now there are diversities of gifts, but the same Spirit. And there are differences of administrations, but the same Lord. And there are diversities of operations, but it is the same God which worketh all in all. But the manifestation of the Spirit is given to every man to profit withal. For to one is given by the Spirit the word of wisdom; to another the word of knowledge by the same Spirit; To another faith by the same Spirit; to another the gifts of healing by the same Spirit; To another the working of miracles; to another prophecy; to another

discerning of spirits; to another divers kinds of tongues; to another the interpretation of tongues: But all these worketh through one and the selfsame Spirit, dividing to every man severally as he will" (1 Cor. 12:4-11).

A close look at the gifts, and their attributes and operations, leads me to submit that the gifts that are most closely tied to dreams, visions, and their interpretations are the word of wisdom, the word of knowledge, prophecy, and discerning of spirits. In this discussion, the believer must understand that the gifts of the Spirit are emanations of the Father that are shed abroad in the believer's heart and mind. They are intended to be used for the edification of the saints. When Paul declares that the gifts are "given to every man to profit withal," he is clearly conveying to the believer that they are dynamic. In other words, by nature, the gifts are vigorously active, filled with divine energy, work progressively to produce change, and are endued with the power of the Most High God himself.

Word of Wisdom: A Supernatural Revelation of Divine Purpose[7]

The predictive elements of dreams, vision, angelic visitations, and the prophetic word represent the revelation of an event in the divine mind. The word of

91

wisdom is used to warn and guide by disclosing future acts of God; to reveal God's will and plan; for assurance of blessings and coming deliverance; to extend God's grace; and to declare divine mysteries.

Word of Knowledge: A Supernatural Revelation of Facts in the Divine Mind[8]

Facts, hidden from the senses, are revealed to us through the word of knowledge. When the Lord Jesus exposed the condition of the churches, as recorded by the Apostle John in Revelation, he was receiving facts from the mind of God. The word of knowledge, to be sure, is a mighty source for effectual, fervent prayer. This gift, illustrated by the revelation of Jesus Christ to the seven churches, is used for the purposes of exhortation. The biblical record also reveals it providential use in specific circumstances to warn Elisha of Syria's secret plan of attack (2 Kings 6:9-12). The Spirit encouraged Elijah with a word of knowledge that he was not alone in his struggle against Baal (1 Kings 19:14-18). It was also used to expose a hypocrite (2 Kings 5:20-27); convict a sinner (Jn. 4:18, 19, 29); discover someone's hiding place (1 Sam. 10:22); reveal corruption (Acts 5:3); and to know the thoughts of men (Jn. 2:24; 1 Sam. 9:19).

Prophecy: A Supernatural Utterance in a Known Tongue[9]

Prophecy in Greek means to "speak for another" and allows the believer to be the Lord's mouthpiece. In Scripture, it is regarded as the most profitable among the gifts. Prophecy can be written, but is most often seen in the contemporary setting as God's use of the vocal chords to speak to men, women, and children. It is meant to edify or build up, and to exhort, comfort, and teach the believers "while its effect upon unbelievers was to show that the secrets of a man's heart are known to God, to convict of sin, and to constrain to worship (vv. 24, 25)."[10] Prophetic messages may be mystical or beyond the realm of the understanding of the vessel being used by God to speak. When the prophetic utterance constitutes a judgment or warning of impending future events, then the gift of prophecy is being used by the Lord as a vehicle for the word of wisdom.

Discerning of Spirits: A Supernatural Insight into the Realm of Spirits[11]

A veil separates the natural from the supernatural. Scripture clearly reveals that, beyond the realm of sight, there exists a world made up of spirits which cannot be seen with the natural eye. The gift of discerning of spirits is a supernatural endowment which allows the believer to see the character and activity of those beings which operate behind the veil. "We need the gift of distinguishing between spirits to help us not only to know what we cannot know otherwise, but also to do something about it — for that is the implication of the knowledge."[12] The gift is God's mechanism to deliver the afflicted, oppressed, and tormented; to discover a satanic emissary; to reveal a scheme, strategy, or device of the enemy; to expose error; and to expose counterfeit miracles. Contrary to the confused beliefs of some, it is not spiritual thought-reading, psychological insight, or keen mental penetration.

I was once interceding for a church that had been in existence only one year. It had rented two small rooms on the second floor of a building owned by the Masonic Lodge. Directly overhead, on the third floor, was the Lodge's temple which could only be accessed by a stairway down the short corridor in front of the church's main entrance. While praying intensely one Tuesday morning, the Lord gave me a vision of an extremely large and powerful demon standing guard at the base of the stairway leading up to the temple.

Across the banisters was a sign that read, "No Entrance." The demon pointed at me and said, "That far and no farther. This building belongs to me!" He then started laughing maniacally. The scene vaporized before me. From beginning to end, the vision lasted less than 60 seconds.

I did not know much about the Masons prior to that experience, except that intense debate had recently broken out at the Southern Baptist Convention over affiliations with the Lodge. I had also known that many earnest Christians regarded them as a secret cult. What concerned me the most was the manifestation of some unusual problems among church members. There had also seemed to be some intimidating presence that kept the church from growing and prevented visitors from coming back.

In less than one minute, during which the Lord briefly lifted the veil, a host of questions were answered and the power of prayer was properly redirected. The Lord supernaturally underscored the necessity to stand on Ephesians chapter six. Once that was accomplished, it was just a matter of months before the church began to experience powerful breakthroughs in the natural.

A Prophetic Warning

Horton makes a statement about prophecy which, I believe, we can extend to all the gifts and represents a strong note of caution worth taking to heart.

> "Such a lovely gift we may be sure will provide much occasion for the cunning manipulation of the enemy. Since he cannot dam so rich a stream, that has begun to flow again from under the holy threshold this wonderful quarter of a century, he will divert it or vitiate it or slander it or exalt it, or in some other way reduce its authority or attractiveness or usefulness or appeal."[13]

On several occasions, I have attempted to emphasize that the field of dreams and dream interpretation is a valuable commodity to the powers and principalities of darkness. I can not over emphasize the fact that we are all involved in a very high stakes battle for the hearts and souls of men, women, and children. In this war, the enemy has had incredible success at pulling countless well-meaning individuals into the riptides of demonic deception characterized best by the New Age dream weaver. We are not to be deceived by appearances. Even though the techniques and paraphernalia promoted by New Age dream enthusiasts seem utterly harmless to the uninformed and

96

uninitiated, we have been instructed that they represent titillating lures into, what is for the Christ-follower, a forbidden world.

The activities of the Kingdom of Darkness are designed to short-circuit an individual's relationship with God by getting him to identify with anything other than Jesus Christ. How a person perceives himself is critical since it correlates directly to how he acts. No person can behave in ways that are inconsistent with the manner in which he views himself. Attitudes, responses, and reactions to the circumstances of life are determined by self-perception. Identity is the sum total of these characteristics and, therefore, becomes a critical ingredient to spiritual warfare. A loss of proper perspective keeps believers separated from Christ and in a state of spiritual defectiveness. Because the gifts of the Spirit are meant to glorify God, the enemy's primary goal in his relentless attacks is to divert and appropriate them for his own purposes. If Satan can accomplish this, he is able to rob glory from God, and that is, after all, what matters the most to him.

Expanding on
the Interpretive Process

We begin with the assumptions that a dream of divine origin is a "speaking forth"; that the process of dream interpretation must depend upon the Holy Spirit; and that the interpretive process is best employed in an atmosphere of a "multitude of counselors" permeated by an understanding of and acceptance for the gifts of the Spirit. With this as a foundation, I will expand on the interpretive process by following three main threads. First, the application of a dream or vision must be considered in light of our relationship with God, our family, and the church. Second, there must be an understanding of the way God speaks. Third, we must comprehend the importance of sound stewardship.

Spheres of Application

In order of importance, a man's relationship are organized with God at the zenith, wife and immediate family second, and ministry and the church third. With this in mind, a prophetic word spoken through a dream or vision can apply to a specific sphere of influence or to all of them simultaneously. It has been my

98

experience that an individual who is interceding diligently for the church may be given valuable light about recent problems, current circumstances, or impending challenges. Since the intercessor is often entangled in the situation pertinent to the dream or vision, it is likely apply to all three spheres of influence: the immediate group of involved individuals, the intercessor himself and, by extension, his family.

Prophetic Terminology

Discourses on prophetic terminology generally pertain to the way God speaks. In dreams, visions, and the prophetic word, there is often confusion about the way time is expressed. We must understand the God operates in *kairos* time, while man operates in *chronos*. Once again we turn to W.E. Vines to make the distinction.

TIME[14]

CHRONOS denotes a space of time, whether short, e.g., Matt. 2:7; Luke 4:5, or long, e.g., Luke 8:27; 20:9; or a succession of times, shorter, e.g., Acts 20:18, or longer, e.g. Rom. 16:25, R.V., "times eternal"; or duration of time, e.g., Mark 2:19, 2nd part, R.V., "while" (A.V., "as long as"), lit., "for whatever time."

Chronos it the time characterized the plodding movement of our clocks, second by second, minute by minute, and hour by hour.

SEASON[15]

KAIROS, primarily, due measure, fitness, proportion, is used in the N.T. to signify a seasons a time, a period possessed of certain characteristics, frequently rendered "time" or "times". . . The characteristics of a period are exemplified in the use of the term with regard, e.g., to harvest, Matt. 13:30; reaping, Gal. 6:9; punishment, Matt. 8:29; discharging duties, Luke 12:42; . . . the fulfillment of prophecy, Luke 1:20; Acts 3:19; 1 Pet. 1:11; a time suitable for a purpose, Luke 4:13."

On the other hand *kairos* is characterized by the sensation everyone has experienced in which an hour feels like a day or a day feels like an hour. Kairos is not hemmed in nor shaped by our clocks. Therefore, when events transpire according the prophetic timetable which occur in a day, we realize that a day, in biblical language, could be 38 years (1 Sam. 15:38). "When personal prophecy comes forth, it is divinely decreed and established in the spiritual, heavenly realm. But it may be many years before it is fulfilled in the natural realm."[16] When dreams express specific time periods, we must not make the mistake of making a literal application unless, of course, the Holy Spirit informs us that was His intention.

Stewardship

What you do with what you learn is as important as what you learn. Scripture clearly teaches us that stewardship is a critical ingredient of His providential care for mankind. From God's instructions to the first couple in Eden to the admonition not to remove nor add a word from Scripture in the last chapter of Revelation, proper stewardship is critical.

> "His lord said unto him, Well done, thou good and faithful servant: thou hast been faithful over a few things, I will make thee ruler over many things: enter thou into the joy of thy lord" (Matt. 25:21).

The gifts of the Spirit, as well as dreams and visions prosper in environments where they are taken viewed soberly and used correctly. They may be taken seriously and misinterpreted, or interpreted properly but never used. The Lord may just be conveying information for the purpose of heightening our awareness of potential trouble or testing our stewardship. If the purpose is not accomplished, we deny God an opportunity to be glorified.

101

The fostering of dreams and visions occurs when the process of reception, interpretation, and proper application takes place from beginning to end as God intended it. God is patient and understands that spiritual growth parallels physical growth. We usually must crawl before we walk. If dreams are not taken seriously, they will never be anything more than a curiosity.

Endnotes

1. Website at "...lite.westal.com/webstuff/defaul3.html."
2. Hal Lindsey, *There's a New World Coming*, (Eugene, OR: Harvest House Publishers, 1973), p. 7.
3. Francis Frangipane, *The Three Battlegrounds* (Cedar Rapids, IA: Arrow Publications , 1989), p 1.
4. Neil Anderson, *The Bondage Breaker* (Eugene, OR: Harvest House Publishers, 1993), p. 79.
5. Denise Linn. The *Hidden Power of Dreams* (New York, NY: Ballantine Books, 1988), p. 84.
6. Harold Horton, *The Gifts of the Spirit* (Springfield, MO: Gospel Publishing House, 1934), p. 24.
7. Ibid., pp. 54-68.
8. Ibid., pp. 39-53.
9. Ibid., pp. 158-176.
10. W.E. Vines, *Vine's Expository Dictionary of New Testament Words* (Oliphants, Ltd., 1940), "P" at p 221.
11. Harold Horton, *The Gifts of the Spirit* (Springfield, MO: Gospel Publishing House, 1934), pp. 69-78.

12. David Linn, *Spiritual Gifts: A Fresh Look* (Springfield, MO: Gospel Publishing House, 1991), p. 80.
13. Harold Horton, *The Gifts of the Spirit* (Springfield, MO: Gospel Publishing House, 1934), p. 159.
14. W.E. Vines, *Vine's Expository Dictionary of New Testament Words* (Oliphants, Ltd., 1940), "T" at p. 138.
15. Ibid., "S" at p. 332-333.
16. Bill Hamon, *Prophets and Personal Prophecy* (Shippensburg, PA: Destiny Image Publishers, 1987), p. 122.

103

For the vision is yet for an appointed time, but at the end it shall speak, and not lie: though it tarry, wait for it; because it will surely come, it will not tarry.

Habakuk 2:3

5

Dreams, Visions, and the Prophetic Word in Panorama

For an individual who recognizes that dreams, visions, and the prophetic word are valuable, he may realize that can be valuable to put them together in a cohesive whole. The Spirit often reveals crucial information progressively, across a period of time. Combined with accurate research; it is possible to create a narrative which has a powerful potential to convey spiritual realities. Frank Peretti's *This Present Darkness*[1] and Rick Joyner's *The Final Quest*[2] are two prominent examples of how the prophetic insights of dreams and visions can be framed to encourage millions. In the short story below, I demonstrate how a combination of dreams, visions, the prophetic word, actual fact, local library research, and a measure of speculation can be woven together into a "fictional" narrative rich with spiritual insights.

THE TRIUMPH OF THE CHOSEN

"For we wrestle not against flesh and blood, but against principalities, against powers, against the rulers of the darkness of this world, against spiritual wickedness in high place" (Eph, 6:12).

Long before organized Christianity became a part of the life of Harford County, Native Americans invoked the spirits of darkness and paid homage to their spirit master through rituals which resemble the New Age magic of their descendants. Witchcraft and satanism are on the rise along the Susquehanna. The same wickedness responsible for the diabolical madness so obvious today was conjured up to engage in spiritual subterfuge by the intoning of mystics in ages past. Principalities move with iron-fisted determination.

There is Method to His Madness

Kosmoskrator Lucifer rules absolutely over a kingdom divided against itself. The only place it is united is deep within his loins. And the binding factor which holds the tendons together is hatred, manifested by devices, schemes, and strategies.

Nowhere is Lucifer's earthly throne revealed. Yet it is situated where it always has been — on the exact spot whereupon once stood the Tree of Life. When Holy God removed the tree to the third heaven and banished the original couple, he waited. In the annals of history, the Garden's location was forever lost, but therein is now seated the center of the Kingdom of Darkness. In Lucifer's eyes, it has been a perpetual symbol of his victory against Jehovah God.

The divisions within his kingdom he himself created with a grand design that is a perversion of the created order. A natural tension gives him the ability to maintain order. He rules by terror. Although he might disguise himself as a ray of light, if a fellow could follow the ray to its source, he would find a bloodthirsty hollowness that curdles the soul.

After The Fall, the human race divided into clans. Outward from the Middle East, they roamed the face of the planet. Some, over countless generations, moved Northward through Asia, across a land bridge, and onto the parcel of land now called North America. Sometimes settling, but more often moving, clans gradually extended themselves as far East as the Atlantic Ocean.

The earliest settlers on the North American continent came to be known as Indians. The word "Indian" mimics the Hebrew name of one of Lucifer's chief princes. In his grand design, Lucifer designated spirit lords to rule over the clans. As small groups settled, subtlety was deftly used to deposit the name of the lords into the hearts and minds of the people. And so they began identifying themselves with the name of the dark power which controlled them. Every time the name was mentioned, the spirit lords received worship unto themselves.

Worship, in any form, gives the powers and principalities of the Enemy's kingdom strength. The more worship a spirit ruler receives, the more power and influence he has. Hence, recognition in Lucifer's kingdom arises out of a spirit's ability to conjure up worship. Across eons, they have become experts at treason, deception, bribery, terror, intimidation, and extortion. Though alliances may be formed, there is no such thing as friendship. At the bottom of it all is intense fear, for Lucifer himself has created an abyss for those who are disloyal. His palace guards stand over the entrance.

There are times, however, when out of the abyss, Lucifer releases one of the condemned to prove himself once more.

Suskwanok

Iskoba moved through the walls of the Harford County Detention Center and ascended in a jet stream through the ceiling, out into the cold blue sky, and began a flight pattern North toward his enclave in Havre de Grace. As he shot through the ether, he wretched with laughter at the scene he had just provoked. They were still arguing about the death of that young man. Human carnage was his specialty and the loss of this particular life had created such turmoil in the County of Harford's government that such explosions were still easily kindled. He revelled at the new plan which was dramatically unfolding. Anger is such a good motivator, he thought!

As Iskoba sailed over Deer Creek, he spied the angelic host standing guard over the King and Queen Seat. One day, he knew in his heart, that parcel of ground would be reclaimed for his principality. Yet, it was vexing to see the warrior Paran entrenched with his cohort on the very ground upon which so many

111

chants and dirges of adoration were offered up to his master, Suskwanok.

For the time being Suskwanok's Minion could no longer assemble at the King and Queen Seat. A new site was chosen to breath together deep beneath the Susquehanna River, on the Havre de Grace side of the Hatem Memorial Bridge. There, Suskwanok and his Minion, of which Iskoba was a chief captain, would strategize, scheme, and design, hatching always what he apprehended to be perversely beautiful blueprints for diabolical madness.

One of Iskoba's favorite exercises were the Minion's forays through the principality which took place on the morning of the first day of every week. It had become a ritual among the Minion to rip and cut through the County of Harford each Sunday morning dismantling the homes of God's children. Multitudes of so-called saints persuaded themselves to stay away from the worship centers through the Minion's carefully crafted chaos. In one swoop, with a loyal contingent of the horde following closely behind him, Iskoba was easily able to deftly sweep through at least five hundred homes stirring up dissent and confusion. He chortled with glee at his ability to successfully pit the saints of God against one another, causing them to fume and

;pit, and even curse the one they call their Lord.

Without a doubt, whoever is given the greatest worship in a given region holds the power and Iskoba would testify that Suskwanok held dominion. Even though those contemptible Christians incessantly waged battle against the Minion, Suskwanok had held unwavering control of this principality for many centuries. Iskoba could recall, as if it were yesterday, how the native Americans would worship Suskwanok with great enthusiasm, often collectively for many days at a time with dance, musical instruments, and ceremonies of all kinds. Eight-day-old infants were baptized into Suskwanok's human family in Deer Creek. A succession of Indian chieftains imbibed by Suskwanok's presence sat upon the King and Queen Seat and governed worship and tribal council meetings, and received ritualistic murder and suicide as alms. So powerful has been Suskwanok's presence that the mighty river which flows through the land was named after him and the Indians themselves came to be known as the Susquehannocks. Suskwanok's name means "spoils obtained in war." So, it was very appropriate that the Indians were called the "people of booty." To this day whenever the name Susquehanna is mentioned, even in passing, the Minion is strengthened.

113

Though no historian is able to document what became of the people of booty, Iskoba knew. He had been standing by Suskwanok's side since Satan himself anointed the demon plenipotentiary and gave him the land now called Harford as his principality. The people of booty, though decimated as a tribe by pestilence and violence, survived through mixed marriages. Today their descendants can be found thriving in covens throughout the County of Harford, knowingly and willfully aiding and abetting, through witchcraft, astrology, channelling, and black magic, in the outworking of Suskwanok's strategems. In fact, it appeared to Iskoba that the people of booty were gaining in strength and stature. The Minion's scouts were picking up a renewed fervor from among the people for the gifts Suskwanok promised all who would fall down before him in worship. Across the County, the blood of animals regularly washed brazen altars in ritualistic sacrifice. With the chants and dirges cleaving to the spilled blood, the Minion became increasingly hopeful that the glory days when Suskwanok sat on the King and Queen Seat would return once again in all their splendor.

Iskoba sailed across the sky, and then, abruptly, slowed his advance, and began to descend into the demonic enclave.   Deep below the river in an underground cavern noted for its total darkness, Suskwanok sat before his Minion receiving the blasphemy from their lips as a sweet fragrance in which he pridefully basked. The more they sang, the larger his breasts grew, the heavier his breathing got, and the more those bulbous orbs set deep in his head would bulge.

Suskwanok began to speak.

"Minion, Suskwanok has just returned from an in-gathering of principalities at which the Great One called Satan appeared. The Serpent has demanded that I turn the Church in my dominion upside down and bring every saint of God to their knees screaming for mercy. You see, Minion, the Serpent has received word that a plan is being hatched by God's vile and despicable saints which, if successful, would strike an extraordinary blow to the Serpent's kingdom. This plan *must* be crushed *now*!   In the midst of the world's principalities, the Serpent lurched at me — he said this grisly thing is being hatched right here! Suskwanok was mocked and taunted for not knowing. Then, the torrid affair about the cohort at the King and Queen Seat was thrust in my face."

Suskwanok let out a bellow that shook the earth beneath the enclave. Anger rose from among the demonic horde. How could this be?

"Minion," Suskwanok roared, "I release you to squeeze those detestable Christians until they choke on the name of their Lord. Stop at nothing!"

The Master of the County of Harford shot his arm to the sky and discharged the horde like lightning from his presence, up and out of the enclave. Left behind were Iskoba and the other chief captains.

"Captains, we must reclaim our ground now. The battle has just begun! But the Christians must not know. How good it is that they are sleeping and disunited. May they suffocate in their lethargy and we be rid of them quickly. Now, go, and do what you do best!"

Quan-Twon

The palace guards threw open the door to the abyss and Lucifer bellowed, "Quan-Twon, I demand your presence!"

From deep within the belly of the earth, wherein molten lava bubbles and foments with intensity that

116

cannot be described, a voice of anguish erupted, "What is it, my lord?"

"Now."

In a flash, a vapor shot up from the pit with a stench that reminded Lucifer of the day he was hurdled across the heavens toward paradise.

"Ready yourself, Quan-Twon," declared Lucifer. "I am sending you as a plenipotentiary of the kingdom to establish a newly created force on the banks of the United States."

"I am at your service, Master. Speak and I shall fly."

Lucifer continued, "You are to go to a place called Grace Harbor and make contact with Suskwanok, my servant, and await instruction."

A roar exploded that shook the ground beneath them. Quan-Twon wailed, "S-u-s-k-w-a-h-a-n-n-o-c-k!!! Arrrgh." Even the palace guards raised their shields as a defense against the Chinaman. The names Quan-Twon and Suskwanok struck horror in the kingdom. Both had mastered with diabolical ruthlessness the ways of the kingdom of darkness. Archenemies within the kosmos, Suskwanok had once overpowered Quan-Twon in a mighty battle at Babylon, and Quan-Twon was forcibly carried into the

117

great abyss.

Lucifer stretched forth his arm and commanded silence with a seething determination that immediately settled the outraged Quan-Twon. "When you arrive, Suskwanok will know by your presence that you appear at my charge. Learn about the land. Study the people. I will send messengers from the Akashic archives and troops from the far reaches of the planet. You will know my plan when the time is right."

To be continued. . .

The short story above pulled together a series of dreams, visions, and prophetic words into a coherent whole. Since the writing ceased, a great many more have been added which, in time, will be worked into the story line. I have chosen three dreams out of many to briefly demonstrate how the method of discovering the hidden meaning dreams set forth in Chapter 4 is able to yield meaningful results.

Extending the Vision
through Dreams

As a pastor who appreciates the light of God as it is shed abroad in the hearts and minds of believers through dreams, visions, and the prophetic word, I put together the method for interpretation just delineated and have attempted to apply it with integrity. One thing that must be stressed. If you have not received an answer to a dream's meaning, resist the urge to create. You may not know some things for years. Let me share a few examples from the intercessory prayer team which has labored with me in ministry.

Dream #1

After recording the dream and following the interpretive process outlined in Chapter 4, begin by making general observations.

> I was on a planet where the people dressed in black and were very strict, authoritarian, and legalistic. A space ship landed, apparently from another planet. These individuals were dressed in varied colors, all light and bright. A lot were young children. Some showed little sexual inhibition. One woman was pregnant. She came to see if she could obtain the release of her spouse. She was told she would have to kill a giant.

119

She crawled into a camel colored tube shaped lake a long
bongo drum that had a canvas top over it. She carried a sword
or dagger with her.

The setting of the dream is "a planet" and there is no
use of "I" which might demonstrate the personal
involvement of the dreamer. Into a bondage-like
situation, alien liberators are introduced. A husband of
one is being held hostage. The liberators are
associated with bright colors, in contrast to the
surrounding darkness, and are mostly youthful. The
allusion to sexuality, along with the fact that one
woman is pregnant, suggests that the aliens are ready
to colonize. Only the woman is prepared to wage
warfare, but is seen going into hiding.

It was apprehended, after prayer, that because the
dream was birthed by a woman whose main function in
the Body of Christ is interceding for the church, that
it was somehow related to the church's ministry. The
authoritarian and legalistic power structure of the
planet represented the spirit of religion. Liberators
were being sent with youthful vigor and, along with
them, new ministries were to be birthed. However, this
would not take place without struggle.

Since the Word of God says, "For the weapons of
our warfare are not carnal, but mighty through God to

120

the pulling down of strong holds" (2 Cor 10:4), I looked to Scripture to determine what the sword and dagger might mean. I found my answer in one of Paul's letters: the "sword of the Spirit, which is the word of God" (Eph. 6:17). The sword he compares the Word to is really a small cut-and-thrust dagger used by Roman warriors.

The covered tube that looked like a bongo drum, into which the woman crawled with her weapons, represents a praise and the canvas top represents God's protection. Praise is a potent weapon which, in the Bible, is seen being used alongside the sword. "Let the high praises of God be in their mouth, and a twoedged sword in their hand; To execute vengeance upon the heathen, and punishments upon the people" (Psa. 149:6-7).

Other, seemingly unrelated, prophetic words gave this dream meaning. To wit, the church was held in bondage by a religious spirit. The Lord wants to take it to another level through praise, worship, and spiritual warfare, and will do that by sending reinforcements in the form of young vigorous Christians pregnant with ideas for new ministry.

It has been said that the counterfeit always precedes the genuine artifact. Shortly after this dream was

121

presented, the church experienced an influx of individuals who had a zealous spirit for revival and a lot of new ideas. However, they had no sense of commitment and loyalty, and disappeared as quickly as they came, leaving much damage behind them. Nevertheless, the Lord reaffirmed His word and His promise, and, as of this writing, we hold onto the vision and wait for its fulfillment.

> "For the vision is yet for an appointed time, but at the end it shall speak, and not lie: though it tarry, wait for it; because it will surely come, it will not tarry" (Hab. 2:3).

This dream was primarily a predictive dream that supplied its meaning through symbolism.

Dream #2

This dream appeared to be a warning which used symbolism.

> A group of believers had a lizard like beast trapped; it had on two legs and was green with scales. There was a skip in sequence and then my two little girls were crowned queens. The lizard cajoled them into releasing to him a key which looked like a railroad spike, but was radiant gold. The key was placed on a black metal grate, in the center. When it was

laid face up in the center, something came to life. A black whisker-like tentacle shot out of the grate and wrapped around the bars. The cage came open and up came a man-like beetle. I couldn't see his face, but his black cloak looked as if he had been in a deep freeze for many years. The beetle stared into a mirror. I saw only his back and heard him say, "I've been locked up for a long time and I'm fuming ." The last thing I remember, the lizard was licking and kissing the youngest girl's face.

This dream was very perplexing and there is still much I do not know about it. One thing seemed clear. There are things about the past which are hidden that, if taken out of the "deep freeze," can cause much damage. A lot of work has taken place in and around my place of ministry pertaining to generational sin. After all, we are told that "the LORD thy God am a jealous God, visiting the iniquity of the fathers upon the children unto the third and fourth generation of them that hate me" (Ex. 20:5). The iniquity of our ancestors can and does impact us today. In this dream, there seems to be an inference that there are keys to generational sin, represented by the man-like beetle that had been in a deep freeze for so long. In this dream, the powers and principalities of darkness used the naivety of children to unlock the past.

Dream #3

This is a prima facie dream mixed with symbolism. The lady is known to the dreamer.

> I was in the back of the church with the keys, getting ready to come in. I noticed a lady coming from the house behind the church toward me. She had a piece of paper in her hand with a combination number on it. The lady tried to open the door to the church using the number, but couldn't seem to get in. She tried the roof, and when that didn't work, she came to the back door. I hid in a corner. She looked right at me, but didn't seem to notice me. The lady turned around. I took off up the street. I knew she heard me and would come looking, so I ducked behind some bushes. The funny thing was, I knew she saw me and that I saw her, but she didn't seem to recognize me.

Again, to unlock the meaning of this dream, we take what we know to be true by observation and combine it with light received through prayer and gifting. No attempt is made to define every dream symbol.

This was an inside-looking-out dream in which the dreamer herself was involved. The dream seems to signify that the church was under some form of attack. The "lady" is known to the dreamer, suggesting familiarity, and the fact that she was seen "coming from the house behind" suggests that the attack would not be frontal. The lady had somehow gotten a hold of a combination that did not work, but that did not stop her. When her attempt to enter the building had failed, she tried the roof. This indicates persistence.

The dreamer saw the lady and the lady saw her, but the lady appeared to be oblivious. Some unseen force was at work which kept the dreamer from being detected.

Individually, these dreams would be regarded as wild and might immediately discarded as driftwood in the seas of consciousness. Certainly, these three dreams would never have been put in relationship to one another absent unique circumstances. However, there is a firm belief within the intercessory prayer team that dreams are a potent tool used by God to protect and edify the church. As a result, these dreams were shared in an atmosphere of openness, permeated by the Spirit. Aside from the intercessors themselves, if we back up, there is indeed a common thread which runs through all of them — *spiritual warfare*. The first dream reveals a land held captive invaded by liberators prepared for battle. The second dream reveals the existence of destructive forces that are hidden, waiting to resurface. The third reveals the existence of flesh and blood proxies laying in wait to infiltrate the work of the church. Together, they are strong admonitions to be on guard, ever ready to defend the Kingdom against aggressors intent on destroying the household of faith.

Endnotes

1. Frank E. Peretti, *This Present Darkness* (Wheaton, IL: Crossway Books, 1986).
2. Rick Joyner, *The Final Quest* (Charlotte, NC: Morning Star Publications, 1997).

Conclusion

As you ponder the source and content of your dreams, do not doubt for a moment that they are more than fascinating displays of the subconcious mind. Indeed, through them, God releases valuable information. We need to guard our dreams as precious gifts from God.

New Release from Moriah Press

The Demons Behind the New Age Movement: And How To Defeat Them
(A PRIMER)
by J.D. Kallmyer

A masterful and scholarly look at the New Age Movement
and how it is able to deceive millions.

- Astrology
- Channeling
- Divination
- Druidism
- Familiar Objects
- Hinduism
- Magic
- Mediumship
- Music

- Paganism
- Satanism
- Shamanism
- Talismans
- Tarot
- Wicca
- Witchcraft
- Yoga
- ... and much more

ORDER FORM

Send $4.75 + $1.25 Shipping/Handling to:
Moriah Press, P.O. Box 917, Havre de Grace, MD 21078-0917

Name: _____

Address: _____

City, State, Zip: _____

Additional copies of "Dreams" may be ordered for
$6.95 + $1.50 Shipping/Handling

New Release from Moriah Press

The Demons Behind the New Age Movement: And How To Defeat Them
(A PRIMER)

by J.D. Kallmyer

A masterful and scholarly look at the New Age Movement
and how it is able to deceive millions.

- Astrology
- Channeling
- Divination
- Druidism
- Familiar Objects
- Hinduism
- Magic
- Mediumship
- Music

- Paganism
- Satanism
- Shamanism
- Talismans
- Tarot
- Wicca
- Witchcraft
- Yoga
- . . . and much more

ORDER FORM
Send $4.75 + $1.25 Shipping/Handling to:
Moriah Press, P.O. Box 917, Havre de Grace, MD 21078-0917

Name: _____

Address: _____

City, State, Zip: _____

Additional copies of "Dreams" may be ordered for
$6.95 + $1.50 Shipping/Handling